PARALLEL LIVES

OPRAH WINFREY

Born in 1954

SONIA SOTOMAYOR

Julie Knutson

CHERRY LAKE PRESS

Published in the United States of America by Cherry Lake Publishing
Ann Arbor, Michigan
www.cherrylakepublishing.com

Reading Adviser: Marla Conn, MS, Ed., Literacy specialist, Read-Ability, Inc.
Cover Designer: Felicia Macheske

Photo Credits: © Photoshot/TopFoto/The Image Works, cover, 1 [left]; © Wikimedia Commons/CC0 1.0 Universal/Public Domain Dedication, cover, 2 [right]; © Anonymous/AP/Shutterstock, 5; © Everett Historical/Shutterstock.com, 6; © Featureflash Photo Agency/Shutterstock.com 9; © Charlie Knoblock/AP/Shutterstock, 10; © skodonnell/iStock.com, 12; © Jason Lee/AP/Shutterstock, 14; © Rena Schild/Shutterstock.com, 15; © Per-Anders Pettersson/Getty Images, 16; © Pesky Monkey/iStock.com, 19; © Enrique Arnaiz Lafuente/Shutterstock.com, 21; © Henny Ray Abrams/AP/Shutterstock, 22; © 2B Photographer/Shutterstock.com, 24; © Erin Alexis Randolph/Dreamstime.com, 25; © Courtesy of the White House, 26

Library of Congress Cataloging-in-Publication Data

Names: Knutson, Julie, author.
Title: Born in 1954 : Oprah Winfrey and Sonia Sotomayor / by Julie Knutson.
Description: Ann Arbor, Michigan : Cherry Lake Publishing, [2020] | Series: Parallel lives | Includes bibliographical references and index. | Audience: Grades 4-6
Identifiers: LCCN 2019033405 (print) | LCCN 2019033406 (ebook) | ISBN 9781534159228 (hardcover) | ISBN 9781534161528 (paperback) | ISBN 9781534160378 (pdf) | ISBN 9781534162679 (ebook)
Subjects: LCSH: Winfrey, Oprah—Juvenile literature. | Television personalities—United States—Biography—Juvenile literature. | African American television personalities—Biography—Juvenile literature. | African American women philanthropists—United States—Biography—Juvenile literature. | Sotomayor, Sonia, 1954—-Juvenile literature. | Women judges—United States—Biography—Juvenile literature. | United States. Supreme Court—Officials and employees—Biography—Juvenile literature. | Hispanic American woman judges—Biography—Juvenile literature.
Classification: LCC PN1992.4.W56 K538 2020 (print) | LCC PN1992.4.W56 (ebook) | DDC 791.4502/80922 [B]—dc23
LC record available at https://lccn.loc.gov/2019033405
LC ebook record available at https://lccn.loc.gov/2019033406

Cherry Lake Publishing would like to acknowledge the work of the Partnership for 21st Century Learning, a Network of Battelle for Kids. Please visit www.battelleforkids.org/networks/p21 for more information.

Printed in the United States of America
Corporate Graphics

ABOUT THE AUTHOR

Julie Knutson shares a birth year with Venus Williams, Chelsea Clinton, and Lin-Manuel Miranda. An avid student of history and former teacher, she lives in northern Illinois with her husband and son.

TABLE OF CONTENTS

CHAPTER 1

Welcome to 1954

1954. Two women are born 5 months and 1,176 miles (1,893 kilometers) apart. Both will become known for **overcoming the odds**, making their voices heard, and creating **opportunities**—not just for themselves, but for entire **communities**. One, Oprah Winfrey, is born in rural Mississippi. The other, Sonia Sotomayor, is born in the Bronx, New York.

What was life in the United States like in 1954 for women and people of color? Two cases heard by the U.S. Supreme Court that year show some of the key developments that influenced their lives. These cases helped shape who these women would become.

In 1960, because of angry mobs, a 6-year-old Ruby Bridges had to be accompanied by U.S. Marshals to and from her previously all-white school in Louisiana.

Brown v. Board of Education: In 1954, the Supreme Court ruled that racial **segregation** in public schools was unconstitutional. Since 1896, the policy of "separate but equal" allowed for separate schools for white children and children of color. With *Brown*, the court ruled that separate schools were instead unequal. The decision was an important landmark in civil rights history. It paved the way for a movement to undo racial prejudice and **injustice**, both in and beyond education.

The U.S. Supreme Court was founded in 1789.

***Hernandez v. Texas*:** The Supreme Court decided that Hispanic and Latino people have equal rights under the Constitution. The court stated that the **14th Amendment** protected Hispanic Americans, not just African Americans. The **defendant**, Pete Hernandez, had been tried and **convicted** before an all-white jury in Jackson County, Texas. That courtroom had not had a Mexican American juror in more than 25 years. The Supreme Court said this prevented Hernandez from having a jury of his peers, which was unconstitutional. The case proved key to establishing civil rights protections for Latino individuals and groups.

What is the Supreme Court?

Nine justices, or judges, serve on the U.S. Supreme Court. This is the highest court in the judicial branch of the federal government. Someone who loses a case in a lower court has the right to ***appeal*** *their case to the Supreme Court. It weighs the case against the laws found in the U.S. Constitution.*

CHAPTER 2

Oprah Winfrey (b. January 29, 1954)

Talk show host. Movie star. Publisher, **entrepreneur**, author, and **philanthropist**. Few people can match Oprah Winfrey's success in the entertainment industry. Oprah overcame many difficulties early in life. She was determined to have her voice heard in the world and to listen to the voices of others.

Early Life: Finding a Voice

Oprah Winfrey was born on January 29, 1954, in Kosciusko, Mississippi. She spent her first 6 years on a farm with her grand-parents. They had very little money. Oprah wore homemade dresses fashioned from potato sacks and played with dolls made of corncobs. Their house lacked indoor plumbing, and they had to boil their

Oprah is the first African American woman to become a billionaire.

If Oprah gives her stamp of approval on a product, people want to buy it. Her influence has been called The Oprah Effect.

clothes to wash them. Despite hardship, Oprah was loved and supported. Her grandmother, Hattie Mae, taught her to read, write, add, and subtract. She took Oprah to church services, where the 3-year-old would stand up and preach. By the time she was 4, Oprah earned the nickname "Little Preacher" for her Sunday sermons.

When Oprah was 6, Hattie Mae got sick. Oprah was sent to live with her mother in Milwaukee, Wisconsin. This major life change didn't stop her love of learning. In kindergarten, she wrote a letter asking to be moved to the first grade. The request was accepted.

Throughout her childhood, she traveled back and forth between her mother in Milwaukee and her father, who lived in Nashville, Tennessee. Her father wouldn't settle for grades lower than an A. He required that she read and report on one book a week. One of those books was Maya Angelou's *I Know Why the Caged Bird Sings*. The message Oprah took from it was to believe in your own power.

A Broadcasting First

While still in high school, Oprah landed a part-time job as a radio news reader. In college, she was offered an anchor position on a local television station. She was the first African American woman to deliver TV news to Nashville audiences.

O, The Oprah Magazine launched in the year 2000.

Middle Years: Expressing a Voice

Oprah discovered public speaking in high school. This opened new doors for her. She held a job as a news reader at a local radio station, and her success at speech competitions earned her a scholarship to Tennessee State University. There she studied communications and performing arts. Soon, she was offered a job as a broadcaster for a local news affiliate. Not long after, she accepted a TV reporting job in Baltimore, Maryland. She left college and Tennessee, just before graduating to start this job.

Oprah's time in Baltimore got off to a rocky start. She was accused of being too emotional and having too much **empathy**. She got **demoted**. But a **producer** at the station saw her potential. He gave her another chance, but in a different type of show. Oprah became the host of *People Are Talking*, a new show with a more human focus. It was a perfect match. Audiences loved Oprah's humor and intelligence, and they could relate to her. These qualities didn't go unnoticed. Soon, she was offered a job in an even bigger market: Chicago, Illinois.

The Oprah Winfrey Show gave a national platform to minority groups to talk about their problems.

Oprah thrived as the host of *A.M. Chicago*. In September 1986, the show was renamed *The Oprah Winfrey Show* and became nationally **syndicated**. Her show invited viewers to listen to points of view they might not otherwise hear, on topics they might otherwise avoid. These included race and gender. *The Oprah Winfrey Show* started conversations about these topics both on and off the air. For 25 years, she carried on these conversations before millions of viewers in over 100 countries.

Oprah was awarded the Presidential Medal of Freedom in 2013.

Oprah has given millions of dollars in contributions to charity through her foundation and through grants.

Later Years: Leaving a Legacy

Oprah's father once told her that there are three types of people in the world: "Those that make things happen, those that watch things happen, and those that don't know what's happening." Throughout her career, Oprah has made things happen. Her advocacy for education through book clubs and **scholarships** continues to change views and lives. She encouraged her TV viewers to volunteer and to become activists. They responded by helping those in need with housing and education.

Empowerment Through Education

Oprah's belief in the power of education is reflected in her philanthropy. In 1987, she established the Oprah Winfrey Foundation. The organization aims to support women, families, and children in the areas of education and health care. Through the foundation, she's given scholarships that allow economically disadvantaged students to attend college.

In 2007, the Oprah Winfrey Leadership Academy for Girls opened in South Africa. The school's mission is to "raise future leaders who are able to navigate a variety of social and cultural contexts." These leaders would "remain committed to the development of South Africa and the African continent." Approximately 322 girls in grades 8–12 attend the school.

CHAPTER 3

Sonia Sotomayor (b. June 25, 1954)

As a Supreme Court justice, Sonia Sotomayor remains firmly and proudly **bicultural**. She views belonging to multiple communities as a strength, not a weakness. Education and conversation have played a huge role in her life. As she wrote in her autobiography, "So much of my life story is about how education opened my eyes to the many possibilities of what I could become."

Early Years: Finding a Voice

Sonia was born in the Bronx, New York, on June 25, 1954, to Celina and Juan Sotomayor. Both of her parents had moved there from Puerto Rico during World War II. As a child, she was

Puerto Rico became a U.S. territory in 1898. Many argue it should become the 51st state.

surrounded by a large and proud family. Sonia's mother believed in the power of education. She worked two jobs so that Sonia and her brother could attend Catholic school. Sonia's father struggled with alcoholism and died when she was only 9 years old.

When Sonia was 7, she was diagnosed with type 1 diabetes. One day, her parents got into a fight over who would give Sonia her **insulin**. Sonia stopped the fight by telling her parents that she'd do it herself. She later remembered, "If I needed to have these shots every day for the rest of my life, the only way I'd survive was to do it myself." Her illness posed other challenges. Doctors told her what she could and couldn't hope to do with her life. Some jobs, like police and detective work, were not possible for people with diabetes. Sonia was very upset! She had dreamed of becoming a detective, like her fictional idol, Nancy Drew. Still, she kept her eyes on justice and law. Inspired by the television program *Perry Mason*, she decided she wanted to be a lawyer or a judge.

In middle and high school, Sonia tried to be the best possible student. In fifth grade, she asked a star classmate for study tips and advice. Sonia made these skills a part of her routine. In high school, she participated in **debate** and student government. Intelligent and dynamic, Sonia was encouraged to look beyond the Bronx for college. On her own, she applied to Harvard, Yale, and Princeton, and was admitted to all three.

Nancy Drew was a popular detective in a fictional book series. She made her debut in 1930.

In celebration of Hispanic Heritage Month, Sonia threw the first pitch at a Yankees game in 2009.

Middle Years: Expressing a Voice

In 1972, Sonia packed her bags and books for Princeton University in New Jersey. At that time in the United States, only 10 percent of Latino high school graduates enrolled in college. Princeton only had around 20 Latino students, and the school had just recently begun admitting women. It was a major change for Sonia, and it wasn't without challenges. She felt out of place. Teachers criticized her written work, which blended Spanish and

Sonia Saves Baseball!

The 1994 baseball season is best remembered for what didn't happen. There was no post-season and no World Series. Team owners were trying to reach an agreement with players about their contracts. But the two sides could not agree about pay. So the players went on strike in August 1994. The strike lasted 272 days. As the start of the 1995 season grew closer, owners proposed replacing the striking athletes with other players.

Enter Judge Sonia Sotomayor! In March 1995, the case came before her court. Sonia sided with the players. This helped the two sides reach an agreement. News outlets nationwide declared Sonia the judge who saved baseball.

During her time at law school, Sonia was the editor of the *Yale Law Journal*.

English in sentences. But Sonia didn't quit. She stood up to **discrimination**. She worked on her writing and did social and community work. She also volunteered in the school's Third World Center. When she graduated in 1976, she was at the top of her class. She was even awarded the university's highest honor, the Pyne Prize.

After attending Yale Law School, Sonia worked for the Manhattan District Attorney's Office in New York. Later she joined a private practice. But her judicial dreams hadn't faded. She continued to meet others in her field, and she volunteered with community

In 2009, Sonia became the first Justice to have their swearing-in ceremony televised.

Sonia is famous for saying, "Until we get equality in education, we won't have an equal society."

organizations for fair housing and legal issues. She worked to gain the experience necessary for a judge. In 1991, Sonia was offered a federal judgeship in New York. She became the first Hispanic federal judge in the state, and the first Puerto Rican woman to serve as a judge in a U.S. federal court. She heard cases on financial crimes and arguments. She became known as a strong judge with a focus on the facts. She moved up to the U.S. Court of Appeals in 1997. This put her in the right place for an **appointment** to the highest court in the land.

Later Years: Leaving a Legacy

After 17 years on the federal bench, Sonia became President Obama's pick to fill a Supreme Court seat. The seat had been held by Justice David Souter. Of the 111 judges in the court's history, she was only the third woman and the first Latina justice. She was vocal about her ability to listen to each side of each case. She also recognized the importance of every decision she would reach.

Sonia has served more than 10 years on the Supreme Court. In that time, she has ruled on important constitutional issues, ranging from **immigration** to health care to voting rights. She has created new cultures of inclusivity at the hallowed institution. Everyone is welcome at her annual holiday party, from clerks to custodians. She continues to work with and advocate for her communities and has stayed true to herself in the process.

Women on the Supreme Court

Sandra Day O'Connor (appointed 1981) and Ruth Bader Ginsburg (appointed 1993) ***preceded*** *Sonia on the Supreme Court. In 2010, Elena Kagan was appointed by President Obama, making her the fourth woman to serve as a justice.*

TIMELINE

January 29, 1954
Oprah Winfrey is born in Mississippi.

May 17, 1954
The Supreme Court rules that school segregation is unconstitutional in *Brown v. Board of Education.*

June 25, 1954
Sonia Sotomayor is born in the Bronx, New York.

1972
Sonia enrolls in Princeton University.

1976
Oprah accepts a position with a television station in Baltimore, Maryland.

1976
Sonia graduates from Princeton summa cum laude.

1979
Sonia graduates from Yale Law School. She becomes a public prosecutor in the Manhattan District Attorney's Office.

1984
Oprah moves to Chicago, Illinois, launching her career in a new market.

1985
Oprah earns Academy Award and Golden Globe nominations for her performance in *The Color Purple.*

1986
The Oprah Winfrey Show airs for the first time to national audiences.

1987
Oprah establishes the Oprah Winfrey Foundation.

1991
Sonia is appointed a federal district judge in New York.

1995
Sonia makes headlines for ending the 272-day Major League Baseball strike.

1996
Oprah launches her book club.

1997
President Clinton appoints Sonia to the U.S. Court of Appeals.

2007
The Oprah Winfrey Leadership Academy for Girls opens in South Africa.

2009
President Obama appoints Sonia as a justice of the U.S. Supreme Court.

2011
The last episode of *The Oprah Winfrey Show* airs.

1986

1991

2007

Research and Act

Reading opened doors for Oprah Winfrey and Sonia Sotomayor. Oprah recognized the power of books for imagining new possibilities and sparking conversations. She started a book club that connects viewers around literature. Being in a book club gives you the opportunity to read, write, speak, and listen as part of a community of readers.

Research

Research programs like Global Read Aloud. This program allows readers worldwide to connect around a shared book.

Act

Launch a book club at your school! Ask your peers what they'd like to read. Take turns selecting titles. Host lunchtime meetings to discuss the big themes of the book. Think about what the story tells about the human experience.

Further Reading

Furgang, Kathy. *Oprah Winfrey: Businesswoman and Actress.* New York, NY: Enslow Publishing, 2019.

Kramer, Barbara. *Who Is Oprah Winfrey?* New York, NY: Penguin Workshop, 2019.

McPherson, Stephanie Sammartino. *Sonia Sotomayor: Supreme Court Justice.* New York, NY: Enslow Publishers, 2016.

Moss, Caroline. *Run the Show Like CEO Oprah Winfrey.* Minneapolis, MN: Frances Lincoln Children's Books, 2019.

Stine, Megan. *Who Is Sonia Sotomayor?* New York, NY: Grosset & Dunlap, 2017.

GLOSSARY

14th Amendment (FOR-teenth uh-MEND-muhnt) a change made to the U.S. Constitution that guarantees all citizens equal protections under law

appeal (uh-PEEL) to ask a higher court for a change in a legal decision

appointment (uh-POINT-muhnt) a job someone is chosen for

bicultural (bye-KUHL-chur-uhl) belonging to two groups of people with their own customs and traditions

convicted (kuhn-VIKT-id) found guilty

debate (dih-BATE) a discussion setting at which people express different opinions

defendant (dih-FEN-duhnt) a person charged with a crime

demoted (dih-MOHT-id) given a less important job

discrimination (dis-krim-ih-NAY-shuhn) unfair behavior to others based on differences in race or gender

empathy (EM-puh-thee) having the ability to understand the feelings of another person

entrepreneur (ahn-truh-pruh-NOOR) a person who starts, organizes, and operates a business

immigration (im-uh-GRAY-shuhn) the act of people moving from one country to another to settle there

injustice (in-JUHS-tis) an unfair situation or action

insulin (IN-suh-lin) a hormone that regulates blood sugar

philanthropist (fuh-LAN-thruh-pist) person who gives money to causes that help others

preceded (pree-SEED-id) came before

producer (pruh-DOO-sur) person in charge of making a TV program

scholarships (SKAH-lur-ships) money given to pay for you to follow a course of study

segregation (seg-rih-GAY-shuhn) the practice of keeping people or groups (such as racial or ethnic) apart

syndicated (SIN-dih-kayt-id) sold to a variety of other networks for broadcast

INDEX